HEALING IS A SETTLED ISSUE

Coffee;
Faith cometh by hearing;
and hearing by a rhema word.
James L. Profit

By

James L. Profit, Jr.

Healing is a Settled Issue

Printed in the United States of America by

Christian Services Network
1959 Longs Hill Road
El Cajon, CA 92021
1-800-636-7276

First printing: January, 2002

International Standard Book Number
1-879854-66-X

ACKNOWLEDGMENTS

I'd like to give the following individuals a heart felt and a special thank you for their support and encouragement in helping me to be obedient to the command of God; to be fruitful.

Bishop Grace C. Osborne, D.D.

Dr. A.C. Williams

Dr. Betty Williams

Dr. Rosie Robinson

Pastor Vernon W. Donald, Jr.

Pastor Brian Buggs

Bruce Tucker

Jennifer

Scott Barker

I believe because of your generosity and the Spirit-led obedience that each of you have demonstrated, the jewels contained within these pages will be manifested in your lives.

TABLE OF CONTENTS

FOREWORD

Many church goers believe that healing is a promise given to them by God. Many think that they will get healed if it is the will of God, and still others believe that because God is sovereign, He does not have to adhere to His Word that never changes. Therefore if they are sick and dying because of that sickness or disease, then God knows best, and it was better for that individual to die with that particular sickness or disease. I am not indicating that God does not know what is best for individual lives because He is omniscient. I am simply saying that God's will for you is for you to be healed, if needed, and healthy.

There are many privileges of being in the Kingdom of God and I believe healing is one of those privileges. Throughout this lesson we will examine the Word of God that deals with the healing of one's body.

INTRODUCTION

Divine intervention for physical healing has long been a topic of controversy among the body of believers in Christ since Jesus walked upon the face of the earth. This is mainly due to the lack of knowledge about the mind and heart of God on this subject. It was said that Jesus was not able to do mighty works in His own country, and among His own kin, and in His own house, save that He could only lay His hands on a few sick folk and heal them. To cure this unbelief, Jesus went about teaching in the villages. (Mark 6:4-6) This shows us that God always desires healing, and that people everywhere are receiving healing for their bodies. It does not matter what the ailment might be. God is still the Healer who has not lost any power to heal.

DEDICATION

This book is dedicated to my eldest child, Janeithia S. Profit. She shall bring healing to her generation through the demonstrated power and love by the Holy Spirit.

SECTION I

FACTS ON BODILY HEALING

CHAPTER ONE

FOREVER SETTLED

Healing man's physical body has already been provided and is an issue that is forever settled in the mind of God. Let us look at what the prophet Isaiah said by the inspiration of the Holy Ghost about our healing.

Isaiah 53:1-5 (Amplified):

Who has believed (trusted in, relied upon and clung to) our message [of that which was revealed to]? And to whom is the arm of the Lord been disclosed?
(v.1)

For [the servant of God grew] up before Him like a tender plant, and like a root out of dry ground; He has no form or comeliness [royal, kingly pomp], that we look at him, and no beauty that we should desire Him.
(v. 2)

He was despised and rejected and forsaken by men, a man of sorrows and pains, and acquainted with grief and sickness; and like one from whom men hide their faces He was despised, and we did not appreciate His worth or have any esteem for Him.
(v. 3)

Surely He has borne our grief (sickness, weakness and distresses) and carried our sorrows and pains [of punishment], yet we [ignorantly] considered Him stricken, smitten and afflicted by God [as if with leprosy].
(v. 4)

He was wounded for our transgress-sions, He was bruised for our guilt and iniquities; the chastisement [needful to obtain] peace and well-being for us was upon Him, and with the stripes [that wounded] Him we are healed and made whole.
(v. 5)

The prophet Isaiah asked the question, "Who has believed?" There is an act on the part of man that God requires and it is only "believe".

Hebrews 11:6 says:

...for he that cometh to God must believe that he is, and that he is a rewarder of them that diligently seek him.

Only believe that your healing is an issue that is forever settled.

Surely He bore our grief, and carried our sorrows.

The words "grief" and "sorrows" are words that were translated from the Hebrew word which meant "sickness and disease." The word "grief" is translated 34 times in the Old Testament to mean "sick." With this in mind, we could read this verse of scripture as:

> *Surely He hath borne our sickness, and carried our diseases.*

Not to accept the healing that has been provided by the stripes that Jesus bore on His body is like saying that what He did was not good enough, and demonstrates a lack of appreciation of His worth.

> *He was wounded for our transgressions, He was bruised for our iniquities.*

Again we see words being used that have a broader meaning in the Hebrew text. The word "bruise" in Hebrew means "to crumble; beat to pieces; break; bruise; crush; destroy; smite." It was by this particular phase of Jesus' bodily sufferings that bodily healing was provided to all who could believe and receive.

It makes no sense at all for man to suffer from sickness and disease when Jesus has already paid the price for every man's bodily healing, because by the stripes that He endured, we are healed!

CHAPTER TWO

HEBREW WORDS ON HEALING (BODILY)

The Hebrew word ***rapha*** is translated as "cure; to make whole; heal; healed; healeth; thoroughly healed; physician."

> *...for I am the Lord who heals you.*
> ***Exodus 15:26***

> *...who heals all your diseases.*
> ***Psalms 103:3***

The Hebrew word ***marpay*** is translated as "healing; health; cure; remedy; sound in health; wholesome."

> *For they are life to those who find them, healing and health to all their flesh.*
> ***Proverbs 4:22***

The Hebrew word ***yeshuwah*** is translated as "health; deliverance; salvation."

The entire 91st Psalm teaches perfect physical health and healing.

The Hebrew word ***arubah*** means "restoration to sound health."

> *Is there no balm in Gilead? Is there no physician there? Why then is not the*

health of the daughter of my people restored? [Because Zion no longer enjoyed the presence of the Great Physician!]
Jeremiah 8:22 (Amplified)

The Hebrew word ***chabash*** means "healer; to bind up or heal."

Come and let us return to the Lord, for He has torn so that He may heal us; He has stricken so that He may bind us up.
Hosea 6:1 (Amplified)

The Hebrew word ***rifooth*** means "health."

It shall be health to your nerves and sinews, and marrow and moistening to your bones.
Proverb 3:8 (Amplified)

CHAPTER THREE

GREEK WORDS ON HEALING

1. **THERAPEUO** primarily signifies "to serve as a ***Therapon"*** (an attendant) then, "to care for the sick; to treat; cure; heal."

> *And Jesus saith unto him, "I will come and heal him."*
> ***Matthew 8:7***

> *And when he had called unto him his twelve disciples, he gave them power against unclean spirits, to cast them out, and heal all manner of sickness and all manner of disease.*
> ***Matthew 10:1***

> *And they watched him, whether he would heal him on the Sabbath day...*
> ***M ark 3:2***

> *And heal the sick that are therein...*
> ***Luke. 10:9***

2. **IAMA** means "healing or repairing."

> *...to another power to cure diseases by the One Spirit.*
> ***I Corinthians. 12:9 (TCNT)***

3. **IAOMAI** means "to heal"; used to describe physical treatment 22 times.

And he sent them to preach the Kingdom of God and to heal the sick.
Luke 9:2

When he heard that Jesus was come out of Judaea into Galilee, he went unto him and besought him that he would come down and heal his son: for he was at the point of death.
John. 4:47

4. **IASIS** means "healing and cure."

For the man was above forty years old, on whom this miracle of healing was shewed.
Acts 4:22

By stretching forth thine hand to heal.
Acts 4: 30

5. **BUGIANO** means "sound health."

Beloved, I wish above all things that thou mayest prosper and be in health.
3 John. 2

6. **HUGIES** means "healthy, sound and whole."

Then said he to the man, "Stretch forth thine hand."
Matthew 12:13

Insomuch that the multitude wondered, when they saw the dumb to speak, the maimed to be whole...
Matthew 15:31

7. **SODZO** means "to save, deliver, protect, heal, preserve, make whole." It is used 86 times in reference to saving the soul, but in several passages it refers to saving the body and healing it of sickness.

> *And straightway the fountain of her blood was dried up: and she felt in her body that she was healed of that plague.*
> ***Mark. 5:29***

> *The same heard Paul speak: who steadfastly beholding him, and perceiving that he had faith to be healed...*
> ***Acts 14:9***

8. **DIA-SODZO** means "to save and to heal thoroughly; make perfectly whole." It is used to describe the body being healed.

> *And when he heard of Jesus, he sent unto him the elders of the Jews, beseeching Him that He would come and heal his servant.*
> ***Luke 7:3***

Throughout this short study of these Hebrew and Greek words, we can easily come to the conclusion that God wants mankind to be well. In the Old Testament many were healed as they lined up with the commandments of God. God led (through Moses) over one million people out of Egypt and there was not one sick person among them. This is an astounding fact considering that these people had been slaves and had worked in unsanitized surroundings.

Later on, Jesus arrived on the scene, healing all manner of sicknesses and diseases, and then gave that same authority to His disciples. We conclude that the God we serve does not change. If He healed then (and He did), He also heals now, for He is the same God yesterday, today and forever.

SECTION II

WHAT DOES THE WORD SAY?

Have a look at **Matthew 9:1-8:**

And he entered into a ship, and passed over, and came into his own city.
(v. 1)

And, behold, they brought to him a man sick of the palsy, lying on a bed: and Jesus seeing their faith said unto the sick of the palsy, 'Son, be of good cheer; thy sins be forgiven thee.'
(v. 2)

And, behold, certain of the scribes said within themselves, "This man blasphemeth."
(v. 3)

And Jesus knowing their thoughts said, wherefore think ye evil in your hearts?
(v. 4)

For whether is easier, to say, thy sins be forgiven thee; or to Say, arise, and walk? But that ye may know that the son of man hath power on earth to forgive sins, (then saith he to the sick of the palsy,) Arise, take up thy bed, and go unto thine house.
(v. 6)

And he arose, and departed to his house.
(v. 7)

But when the multitudes saw it, they marveled and glorified God, which had given such power unto men.
(v. 8)

The people marveled at the healing, the forgiving of sins, and also marveled and glorified God, who had given such power unto men.

Jesus showed that He had power on Earth to forgive sins by showing that sin and sickness or disease are intertangled together. And by releasing the man from his physical bondage, Jesus in this particular case also released the man from spiritual bondage.

Have a look at **Luke 17:11-19:**

And it came to pass, as he went to Jerusalem, that he passed through the midst of Samaria and Galilee.
(v. 11)

And as he entered into a certain village, there he met him ten men that were lepers, which stood afar off.
(v. 12)

And they lifted up their voices, and said, Jesus, Master, have mercy on us.
(v. 13)

And when he saw them, he said unto them, "Go shew yourselves unto the priests." And it came to pass that as they went, they were cleansed.
(v. 14)

And one of them, when he saw that he was healed, turned back and with a loud voice, glorified God.
(v. 15)

And fell down on his face at his feet, giving thanks: and he was a Samaritan.
(v. 16)

And Jesus answering said, "Were There not ten cleansed? But where are the nine?"
(v. 17)

"There are not found that returned to give glory to God, save this stranger."
(v. 18)

And he said unto him, "Arise, go thy way: thy faith hath made thee whole."
(v. 19)

Here again Jesus heals a person bodily as well as spiritually. The scriptures make it plain that it was a Samaritan who returned to give God thanks. It is important to see this parallel and insinuation that Jesus makes. The Samaritan could have possibly represented the sinner man and the other nine possibly being Jews, represented the people who had the promises of God (Matthew 15:26). The non-Jewish man, after he noticed that his healing had manifested, returned to give God thanks. And Jesus makes the statement "But were there not ten cleansed? But where is the nine?" It seems that Jesus was waiting on all ten to return so all ten would be made whole, not only in bodily healings but also to receive spiritual healing.

John 4:46:

So Jesus came again into Cana of Galilee, where he made the water wine. And there was a certain nobleman, whose son was sick at Capernaum.
(v. 46)

When he heard that Jesus was come out of Judaea into Galilee, he went unto him, and besought him that he would come down and heal his son: for he was at the point of death.
(v. 47)

Then said Jesus unto him, "Except ye see signs and wonders, ye will not believe."
(v. 48)

The nobleman saith unto him, Sir come down ere my child die.
(v. 49)

Jesus saith unto him, "Go thy way; thy son liveth." And the man believed the word that Jesus had spoken unto him, and he went his way.
(v. 50)

And as he was now going down, his servants met him, and told him, saying, Thy son liveth.
(v. 51)

Then inquired he of them the hour when he began to amend. And they said unto him, Yesterday at the seventh hour the fever left him.
(v. 52)

So the father knew it was at the same hour in which Jesus said unto him, Thy son liveth: and himself believed, and his whole house.
(v. 53)

Here again we see salvation coupled with healing. It is obvious that this man's whole house became believers after the son was healed (v. 53). So we can say they were undoubtedly unbelievers. I would also like to point out that the son became a believer because he was part of the whole house, servants included.

Let me also point out that the father expected his son to gradually get better (v. 52), but the response from the servants was "Yesterday at the seventh hour the fever left him", which was the same hour that Jesus had assured the father that his son would live.

Jesus talks about a sower sowing seeds into many different grounds. The grounds represent the different types of hearts that the seed would fall upon. And the seed is the Word of God. Only the ground which is good ground would bring forth fruit, some a hundred-fold, some sixty-fold, some thirty-fold (Matthew 13:1-9).

But Jesus continues to talk about the issue to open the understanding of the disciples concerning what he was talking about in Matthew 13:15.

> *For this people's heart is waxed gross, and their ears are dull of hearing, and their eyes they have closed; lest at any time they should see with their eyes, and hear with their ears, and should understand with their heart, and should be converted, and I should heal them.*

Again, this scripture demonstrates the two-fold blessing that can be received at salvation.

CHAPTER FOUR

Salvation and Healing Are Inseparable

There are several instances in the Old Testament where salvation and healing are found in the same scripture verse. Let us take a look at some of them.

Pslams 103:1-3

Bless the Lord, O my soul, and all that is within me, bless his holy name.
(v. 1)

Bless the Lord, O my soul, and forget not all his benefits.
(v.2)

Who forgiveth all thine ***iniquities****; who* ***healeth all thy diseases.***
(v. 3)

Psalms 107:20

He sent his word and ***healed them****, and* ***delivered them*** *from their destructions.*

Proverbs 4:20-22

My son, attend to my words; incline thine ear unto my sayings.
(v. 20)

Let them not depart from thine eyes; keep them in the midst of thine heart. **(v. 21)**

For they are ***life unto those that find them****, and* ***health to all their flesh.*** **(v. 22)**

Also, I would like you to read Psalm 91. This Psalm depicts a life of dwelling in the presence of God and walking in His divine health so that you might continually see the salvation of the Lord.

Then why is divine health such an overlooked fact?

I would speculate and say it is because the knowledge that has been revealed on this fact is rejected.

The prophet Hosea makes a statement about rejecting the knowledge of God (Hosea 4:6):

My people are destroyed for lack of knowledge: because thou hast rejected knowledge.

To reject the knowledge of God is the same as rejecting God. Therefore, God's response is "I will also reject you."

If we as a people choose not to agree with God's Word, it is impossible to receive the benefits that are given to all the children of God. Amos 3:3 says, *"Can two walk together, except they be agreed?"*

Jesus said,

Any kingdom that is divided against itself is being brought to desolation and laid waste, and no city or house divided against itself will last or continue to stand.
Matthew 12:25 (Amplified)

Jesus also stated, in Matthew 18:19 (Amplified),

Again I tell you, if two of you on earth agree (harmonize together, make a symphony together) about whatever [anything and everything] they may ask, it will come to pass and be done for them by My Father in heaven.

God is looking for agreement. The moment you agree with God concerning healing being a forever settled fact, it will become yours.

Other New Testament scriptures that solidify this truth are:

Matthew 8:17

That it might be fulfilled which was spoken by Esaias the prophet, saying, Himself took our infirmities, and bare our sicknesses.

3 John 2

Beloved, I wish above all things that thou mayest prosper and be in health, even as thy soul prospereth.

These two different writers express that God wants His children healed and healthy.

First and foremost God is concerned with your spiritual prosperity.

II Peter 3:9 (Amplified)

> *...not desiring that any should perish, but that all should turn to repentance.*

He wants you and I to be saved from a place called "Hell" prepared for Satan.

> *[The Father] has delivered and drawn us to Himself out of the control and the dominion of darkness and has transferred us into the kingdom of the Son of His love.*
> ***(Colossians 1:13, Amplified)***

3 John 2 indicates God's desire is that mankind prospers in every area of his life (spiritually, physically, mentally, socially, financially). Prosperity will be of no avail if a man does not get back into right standing with God.

> *For what is a man profited, if he shall gain the whole world, and lose his own soul?*
> ***(Matthew 16:26)***

The primary point is to become a new man who is after God, created in righteousness and true holiness. (Read II Corinthians 5:17; Ephesians 4:24; II Corinthians 5:21)

Life is not truly lived unless it is lived in Christ Jesus being directed by the Spirit of God. To live and not be alive unto the things of God is to be dead and an alien to God.

John 10:10 (Amplified) says,

> *The thief comes only in order that he may steal and may kill and may destroy. I came that they may have and enjoy life, and have it in abundance - to the full, till it overflows.*

The Bible says in the book of **Acts 10:38**,

> *How God anointed Jesus of Nazareth with the Holy Ghost and with power who went about doing good, and healing all that were oppressed of the devil; for God was with him.*

There are two contrasting elements in the scripture just read...good and evil. The scriptures identify the one who is doing good and also it identifies the one who is doing evil. God is good, therefore everything that comes from God is good (James 1:17) and Satan is the oppressor of man as brought out in Acts 10:38.

Read I Corinthians 11:23-32.

Remember, the bread is a symbol of His body. Even as the bread is broken, so was His body marred and beat to pieces so our bodies would not have to be. The cup is a symbol of the New Testament in His blood...blood that was shed for the remitting of sins and sprinkled on the heavenly mercy seat for all of mankind.

Two more references may be worth a look:

I Peter 2:24

> *Who his own self bare our sins in his own body on the tree, that we, being dead to sins, should live unto righteousness: by whose stripes ye were healed.*

The mutilation of Jesus' body is the reason why your and my body can be whole.

James 5:14-16

> *Is any sick among you? Let him call for the elders of the church; and let them pray over him, anointing him with oil in the name of the Lord. And the prayer of faith shall save the sick, and the Lord shall raise him up; and if he have committed sins, they shall be forgiven him. Confess your faults one to another, and pray one for another, that ye may be healed. The effectual fervent prayer of a righteous man availeth much.*

It is without a doubt that God wants people saved and healed, living a life of prosperity. This prosperity begins at the birth of an individual into the Kingdom of God. It does not matter if one gets the body healed and fails to accept Jesus Christ as their Lord, the most important element of life. Let us do first things first...

What will it profit a man if he gains the whole world, (health and healing included) *and lose his soul.*
(Matthew 16:26)

CHAPTER FIVE

Acceptable Speech

After being in church for more than twenty years, I find that there is a language of the local church body and a language of the Body of Christ. These two are totally different from each other and they both get completely different results.

Learning to confess the Word of God concerning any situation is what will produce the desired results. A heart should be filled with the Word of God so there will be no room for doubting, only believing and then speaking forth.

> *We having the same spirit of faith, according as it is written, I believed, and therefore have I spoken; we also believe, and therefore speak;*
> ***(II Corinthians 4:13)***

It is very difficult to get something out of a person's spirit if it is not in them in abundance. What we are accustomed to hearing is what is in a person's head; consequently, the fleshly results follow. Jesus, speaking to the Pharisees of the day, said *"Out of the abundance of the heart the mouth speaks." (Matthew 12:34))*

The Apostle Paul admonished the Ephesian church to be renewed in the spirit of their mind. We know that the Holy Spirit inspired holy men of old to write this, and these words are not exclusively for this particular church but for the whole Body of Christ. (Ephesians 4:23)

It is by our words that we will be justified and it is by our words that we will be condemned. (Matthew 12:37) We should not be conformed to this world (its way of thinking and its way of talking), but be transformed by the renewing of our minds. (Roman 12:2)

The way a mind is renewed to the Word of God is through reading, studying and meditating upon it. Afterwards, the heart will be filled to overflowing, and out of the abundance of the good that has entered your heart the mouth will be able to allow gracious words of life to flow to every dead or dying situation in your environment.

We have a high priest for our confession. The only confessions that He can be High priest over are His own words that we have thoughtfully and attentively put into our hearts. Our speaking concerning any issue should be supported with the Word of God.

> *Wherefore, holy brethren, partakers of the heavenly calling, consider the Apostle and High Priest of our profession, Christ Jesus.* ***(Hebrews 3:1)***

Idle words should not proceed out of the believers mouth, but only words that will produce. Idle words are non-productive words, words that have no life in them, words that are not of faith.

We are to imitate Jesus and speak words that are spirit and life.

It is the spirit that quickeneth; the flesh profiteth nothing: the words that I speak unto you, they are spirit and they are life.
(John 6:63)

Therefore, as imitators of God, our choices are to be words of life.

Words that are not faith producing, life and light-giving will not be acceptable in His sight.

Let the words of my mouth and the meditation of my heart, be acceptable in thy sight, O Lord, my strength, and my redeemer.
(Psalms 19:14)

Here are some other scriptures that emphasize the Word is important and must be watched over and spoken correctly.

Therewith bless we God, even the Father; and therewith curse we men which are made after the similitude of God. Out of the same mouth proceedeth blessing and cursing. My brethren, these things ought not so to be.
(James 3:9,10)

A man shall eat good by the fruit of his mouth.;...He that keepeth his mouth keepeth his life: but he that openeth wide his lips shall have destruction.
(Proverbs 13:2,3)

There is that speaketh like the piercing of a sword: but the tongue of the wise is health.
(Proverbs 12:18)

Who satisfieth thy mouth with good things; so that thy youth is renewed like the eagle's. ***(Psalms 103:5)***

It is obvious through these scripture passages that words we speak cause certain actions and reactions in our lives. Therefore, when it comes to health, prosperity and faith; begin to talk in line with the Word of God to get the God kind of results.

In the beginning God created the heaven and earth. And the earth was without form, and void; and darkness was upon the face of the deep. And the Spirit of God moved upon the face of the waters. And God said, Let there be light; and there was light. And God saw the light, that it was good:
(Genesis 1:1-4)

God created the heavens and the earth using words that were in abundance in His heart. When He spoke the words out, the image that was formed in Him materialized in the natural realm and is still being upheld by that same word.

Who being the brightness of his glory, and the express image of his person, and upholding all things by the word of his power.
(Hebrews 1:3)

We must understand that God has given unto us the same creative ability using His Word because we have been made in His image and after His likeness. (Genesis 1:26)

Therefore as dear children of God we can follow after Him.
(Ephesians 5:1)

These two passages of scripture demonstrate what God expects of His children. Since we are made in His image and after His likeness, it would be rather easy to act like Him. The way one acts like another person is to imitate the person by saying what they hear them say and doing what they see them doing. Therefore, we should fill our hearts with the Word of God, which is God speaking to us. The Bible says holy men of God spake as they were moved by the Holy Ghost. (2 Peter 1:21)

God has given us the words to use in our lives that will cause us to experience good. The only difference between our non-producing words and the productive words of God is that our non-producing words are coming out of minds which have not been transformed by the Word of God. Consequently, we are speaking whatever is in abundance in our hearts.

O generation of vipers, how can ye, being evil, speak good things? For out of the abundance of the heart the mouth speaketh. A good man out of the good treasure of the heart bringeth forth good But I say unto you, that every idle word that men shall speak, they shall give account thereof in the day of judgement. For by thy words thou shalt be justified and by thy words thou shalt be condemned.
(Matthew 12:34-36)

I am fully persuaded that we are expected of God to use words to control our environment.

> *For in many things we offend all. If any man offend not in word, the same is a perfect man, and able to bridle the whole body. Behold, we put bits in the horses' mouth, that they may obey us; and we turn about their whole body. Behold the ships, which though they be so great, and are driven of fierce winds, yet are they turned about with a very small helm, withersoever the governor listeth. Even so the tongue is a little member, and boasteth great things. Behold, how great a matter a little fire kindleth! And the tongue is a fire, a world of iniquity: so is the tongue among our members, that it defileth the whole body, and setteth on fire the course of nature; and it is set on fire of hell. For every kind of beast, and of birds, and of serpents, is tamed, and hath been tamed of mankind: But the tongue can no man tame; it is an unruly evil, full of deadly poison. Therewith bless we God, even the Father; and therewith curse we men, which are made after the similitude of God. Out of the same mouth proceedeth blessing and cursing. My brethren, these things ougth not so to be. Doth a fountain send forth at the same place sweet water and bitter?*
> ***(James 3:2-11)***

CHAPTER SIX

Different Ways of Receiving Healing

There is a difference from receiving healing by the laying on of hands and by the gifts of healing in manifestation. All over this country and countries abroad saints flood the altars at the end of services to get hands laid on them, hoping to receive an immediate healing with Mark 16:18 in their minds which states...

> *They shall lay hands on the sick, and they will recover.*

This scripture is referring to every believer having the right to exercise this covenant, blood-bought right. It also indicates a process of time before the individual gets well (and they will recover). All this is based on the faith of the individual needing healing.

The person who comes to the altar is really expecting a gift to be in operation (the gift of healing or the working of miracles) through the person doing the laying on of hands and needs a physical point of contact (otherwise he or she could receive their healing right where they are standing).

Some might ask, "What is the difference?"

The difference is simple: one works as the Holy Spirit wills (see I Corinthians 12:4-11) and the laying on of hands works as the individual wills by being obedient and exercising their faith.

Every believer has been commanded to lay hands on the sick. We can classify this as a believers anointing. This healing is completely based on the faith of the person needing the healing. The gift of healing is a gift that a minister has been endowed with by the Holy Spirit to minister healing to someone.

The person receiving the healing does not have to exercise his or her faith to receive, because it is an act completely based upon the will of the Holy Spirit. After the person has received their healing it will take the exercising of their faith to maintain the healing. That is why so many people become afflicted with the same ailment after they have received healing. The individual fails to realize that they must do something about keeping their healing.

The gift of healing has to do with bringing one's body back up to its original state of health. Example: There may exist pain in your chest. Someone lays hands on you, rebukes the pain and immediately it disappears. Another example: one leg is shorter than the other one. Someone lays hands on you and command the body to line up in order and for that leg to be the same length as the other one. Now, depending on that leg not having parts missing, it should respond to the command of the believer.

Any manifestation of an immediate healing is an evident token of a gift in operation. The working of miracles is a gift also that takes place immediately, but the uniqueness of this gift is that something has been replaced or recreated, such as a new heart, a new lung or eye.

This is an area that has almost been forgotten, but is looked to for some superstar in the Body of Christ. Remember that God never changes. If He did it in the Old testament and in the early church, He is still doing it today.

> *Jesus Christ the same yesterday, and today and forever.*
> ***(Hebrews 13:8)***

> *Now concerning spiritual gifts, brethren, I would not have you ignorant. Ye know that ye were Gentiles, carried away unto these dumb idols, even as ye were led. Wherefore I give you to understand, that no man speaking by the Spirit of God calleth Jesus accursed: And that no man can say that Jesus is Lord, but by the Holy Ghost. Now there are diversities of gifts, but the same Spirit. And there are differences of administrations, but the same Lord. And there are diversities of operations, but it is the same God which worketh all in all. But the manifestation of the Spirit is given to every man to profit withal. For to one is given by the Spirit the word of wisdom; to another the word of knowledge by the same Spirit; To another faith by the same Spirit; to another gifts of healing by the same Spirit; To another the working of miracles; to another prophecy; to another discerning of spirits; to another divers kinds of tongues; to another the interpretation of tongues: But all these worketh that one and the selfsame Spirit, dividing to every man severally as he will.*
> ***(I Corinthians 12:1-11)***

And, Behold, a woman, which was diseased with an issue of blood twelve years, came behind him, and touched the hem of his garment: For she said within herself, If I may but touch his garment, I shall be whole. But Jesus turned him about, and when he saw her, he said, "Daughter be of good comfort; thy faith hath made thee whole." And the woman was made whole from that hour.
(Matthew 9: 20-22)

Jesus did not lay hands on this woman, but she received her healing because her faith in the touch of his garment (the point of contact) helped her to release her faith, thereby receiving from the heart of God, her heart's desire.

But without faith it is impossible to please him; for he that cometh to God must believe that he is, and that he is a rewarder of them that diligently seek him.
(Hebrews 11:6)

Let us look at another passage of scripture.

And he touched him, saying, I am willing; be cleansed by being cured. And instantly his leprosy was cured and cleansed.
(Matthew 8:3, Amplified)

And he was not able to do even one work of power there, except that he laid his hands on a few sickly people and cured them.
(Mark 6:5, Amplified)

In these passages we see three different healings occurring. In Matthew 9:20-22 it states that the woman receiving healing received by her own faith. The second, in Matthew 8:3, received by the working of miracles, and the third manifestation in Mark 6:5 was the gift of healing.

When a person receives healing based on a gift of the Holy Spirit in operation it will take no faith at all on the person receiving, but it will take faith to maintain their healing. This is one of the main reasons that many saints loose their healings. They fail to understand that they must stand against any attempt of the enemy to give them the sickness or disease from which they had previously been healed.

To receive healing by the laying on of ones hands, the person expecting to receive his healing must receive according to their own faith. Therefore, there might not be an immediate manifestation of the healing being sought after.

More supporting scriptures to read:

> *And they came to Jericho: and as he went out of Jericho with his Disciples and a great number of people, blind Bartimaeus, the son of Timaeus, sat by the highway side begging. And when he heard that it was Jesus of Nazareth, he began to cry out, and say, Jesus, thou son of David, have mercy on me. And many charged him that he should hold his peace: but he cried the more a great deal, Thou son of David, have mercy on me. And Jesus stood still, and commanded him to be called. And they called the blind man, saying*

unto him, Be of good comfort, rise; he calleth thee. And Jesus answered and said unto him, "What wilt thou that I should do unto thee?" The blind man said unto him, Lord, that I might receive my sight. And Jesus said unto him, "Go thy way; thy faith hath made thee whole." And immediately he received his sight, and followed Jesus in the way.
(Mark 10: 46-52)

And it came to pass, as he went to Jerusalem, that he passed through the midst of Samaria and Galilee. And as he entered into a certain village, there met him ten men that were lepers, which stood afar off: And they lifted up their voices, and said, Jesus, Master, have mercy on us. And when he saw them, he said unto them, "Go shew yourselves unto the priests." And it came to pass, that, as they went, they were cleansed. And one of them, when he saw that he was healed, turned back, and with a loud voice glorified God, And fell down on his face at his feet, giving him thanks: and he was a Samaritan. And Jesus answering said, "Were there not ten cleansed? but where are the nine?" There are not found that returned to give glory to God, save this stranger. And he said unto him, "Arise, go thy way: thy faith hath made thee whole."
(Luke 17:11-19)

Section III

Testimonies

The following testimonies are actual occurrences that took place and have been validated by doctor's reports.

Whenever God does a healing of a physical body it will stand up to any scrutinizing.

What God has done for these He is willing and ready to do for you.

CHAPTER SEVEN

Stretch Forth Thy Hand

It happened in a Friday evening service. There was nothing different about this service, a regular, formatted Friday night service. The only difference about tonight was that I had come to receive my healing that the Lord had already provided through the shed blood and stripes of Jesus. See Isaiah 53:4-5.

My name is Rose. I'm a Christian and have been one for more than ten years now. I love the Lord Jesus with all my heart. I had begun to experience some numbness in several of the digits and had lost a considerable amount of strength in my right hand; it was also difficult for me to close my hand up to make a fist. So I decided to make an office call to my primary physician to find out what was happening with my hand. My doctor examined my hand and quickly gave me a diagnosis of having "Carpel

Tunnel Syndrome". He stated that he would have to operate on the nerves in the hand to restore it back to normal.

When the service came to an end, the altar call was given and I went forward to get my healing through the laying on of hands. All I know is that I had come that night to receive because I didn't want the doctor cutting on me. I remember the minister asking, "What do you want the Lord to do for you tonight?" I proceeded to tell him my story. He asked me, "Do you believe that God wants you well?" My response was obviously yes. The minister commanded my hand to be restored to normal in the Name of Jesus. I went back to the doctor's office to find out that God had honored my faith and healed my hand!

This type of healing is not new nor is it unique to any one person. The Lord Jesus encountered a man with a similar case. The man had a withered hand and he received the same results as Rose, because God does not change.

> *And it came to pass also on another Sabbath, that he entered into the synagogue and taught: and there was a man whose right hand was withered. And the scribes and Pharisees watched him, whether he would heal on the Sabbath day; that they find an accusation against him. But he knew their thoughts, and said to the man which had the withered hand, "Rise up, and stand forth in the midst." Then said Jesus unto them, "I will ask you one thing; Is it lawful on the Sabbath days to do good, or to do evil? To save life, or*

to destroy it?" And looking round about upon them all, he said unto the man, "Stretch forth thy hand." And he did so and his hand was restored whole as the other.

Matthew, Mark and Luke all made mention of this episode of healing. The main point in this passage of scripture was not the healing of the withered hand but the understanding of what the will of the Father is concerning those who come to him in faith on any day.

CHAPTER EIGHT

Breast Cancer Healed

My name is Joyce and I am an active member at one of the local Christian congregations in the city of San Diego. My story began in the year of 1985 when doctors diagnosed me with breast cancer. At the guidance of my primary physician, I underwent the necessary operation to save my life. In the latter part of the year of 1990 I was given grievous news that the cancer was back again, this time in the other breast. The doctor told me to return in 6 months. During this time I had made up my mind to receive healing that Jesus Christ had so long ago paid for. Two weeks before my return to the hospital I came to church on a Sunday morning. As the preached word went forth, my faith was built up even more. (See Romans 10:17)

The regular portion of the services ended and the pastor made an altar call for those who wanted to give their lives to Christ. I waited patiently for him to make the call for those who needed and wanted to be healed of any sickness or disease. When the call was made I was one of the first ones to move toward that altar.

I knew that my healing was shortly coming.

As I stood before the minister, he asked me, "What do you want the Lord to do?" I began to relate my story to him about my bout with this cancerous disease that keeps returning. The minister quoted scriptures that indicated that we have authority over sickness and disease, and then he rebuked the cancer as if he were talking to a person and commanded the cancerous disease to die and to leave my body. I returned to the hospital for another monogram to find that the cancer was no where to be found! When the doctor gave me the negative results of the test, I knew it was the healing touch of the Lord Jesus that had made me whole.

Throughout the Gospels, Jesus commanded situations to change. We can see in scripture that we are admonished to imitate God (See Ephesians 5:1) and command sickness and disease to obey.

And when Jesus was entered into Capernaum, there came unto him a centurion, beseeching him, And saying, Lord, my servant lieth at home sick of the palsy, grievously tormented. And Jesus said unto him, "I will come and heal him." The centurion answered and said, Lord, I am not worthy that thou shouldest come under my roof: but speak the word only, and my servant shall be healed. For I am a man under authority, having soldiers under me, and I say to this one, Go, and he goeth; And to another, Come, and he cometh; and to my servant do this, and he doeth it. When Jesus heard it, he marveled, and said to them that followed, "Verily I say unto you, I have not found so great faith, no, not in Israel." [Verse 13) And Jesus said unto the centurion, "Go thy way; and as thou hast believed, so be it done unto thee."
(Matthew 8:5-10,13)

This occurrence is for our benefit, showing the believers that we have positional authority over sickness and disease.

> *Behold, I give unto you power* (the Greek word for power is "Exousia"...meaning "delegated authority") *to tread on serpents and scorpions, and over all the power of the enemy: and nothing shall by any means hurt you.*
> ***(Luke 10:19)***

This makes the position of a believer more clearly seen over sickness, disease and Satan in the Name of Jesus Christ of Nazareth. Jesus was manifested to destroy the works of the devil and sickness and disease originate from the devil. See I John 3:8.

We who are sons of God have been given the right through Jesus' victory over Satan to exercise authority over anything out of the kingdom of darkness, hence enforcing Jesus' victory over Satan.

> *And having spoiled principalities and powers, he made a shew of them openly, triumphing over them in it.* ***(Colossians 2:15)***

CHAPTER NINE

Be Loosed From Your Infirmity

How would you like to have an ailment or an infirmity in your body for many years? The answer is obvious. But the writer Luke identifies a woman who was bound by a spirit of infirmity for eighteen long years.

> *And he was teaching in one of the synagogues on the sabbath. And, behold, there was a woman which had a spirit of infirmity eighteen years and was bowed together and could in no wise lift up herself. And when Jesus saw her, he called her to him, and said unto her, "Woman, thou art loosed from thine infirmity." And he laid his hands on her: and immediately she was made straight, and glorified God.*
> ***(Luke 13:10-13)***

This scripture text was referred to because there was a certain man in the local church bound with pain in his right hip for two long years. As this woman was in the synagogues, so was this man in the church. She had heard the law being taught as this man had and was hearing the Word being preached. Jesus said that the woman was already loosed from her infirmity (being a daughter of Abraham). This man was already loosed from his pain being of the seed of Abraham and a Son of God, but his healing had not manifested in his body. Listen to what Jesus says to the woman in verse 12...*"thou art loosed from thine infirmity."* Yet there was no response nor was there any reaction until Jesus laid His hands upon her and immediately she was made straight.

So it was with this man, until hands were laid upon him the pain was negatively affecting his body causing him to use a cane to get around. As a result of hands being laid upon him, he likewise received his healing and glorified God!

There are many in the body of Christ suffering from afflictions needlessly. Jesus has already paid the price for the health of our bodies. We as Sons of God are freed from anything the enemy tries to put on our bodies.

> *Christ hath redeemed us from the curse of the law, being made a curse for us: for it is written, Cursed is everyone that hangeth on a tree: That the blessing of Abraham might come on the Gentiles through Jesus Christ; that we might receive the promise of the Spirit through faith.*
> ***(Galatians 3:13,14)***

There are many more testimonies that have been documented, and we could print them to encourage you to believe for your healing. Such as a kidney transplant being rejected, but as a result of hands being laid upon the person in the Name of Jesus Christ, his body accepts the transplant. Back discs being healed, arms grown out, legs grown out. One woman was trampled and experienced unbearable pain and stiffness in her neck and back, but after hands were laid upon her, in Jesus Christ Name all pain and stiffness disappeared as she received her healing.

Every man and woman in the Body of Christ has a right to enjoy prosperity in their health. So began to walk in this knowledge that ***Healing is a Settled Issue.***

Epilogue

Sickness and disease are enemies of God! They constantly rob members of the Body of Christ of their right to live healthy lives. Jesus Christ paid the price for every man and woman to be delivered from the curse.

The mode of thinking that hinders one from receiving is the lack of understanding that this fact of healing belongs to the Body of Christ and a lack of knowledge of the fact that ***Healing is a Settled Issue***.

Decision

The Bible says,

> *For all have sinned, and come short of the glory of God.*
> ***(Romans 3:23)***
>
> *For the wages of sin is death; but the gift of God is eternal life through Jesus Christ our Lord.*
> ***(Romans 6:23)***
>
> *Therefore repent and be baptized every one of you in the name of Jesus Christ for the remission of your sins and you shall receive the gift of the Holy Ghost.*
> ***(Acts 2:38)***
>
> *That if thou shalt confess with thy mouth the Lord Jesus, and shalt believe in thine heart that God hath raised him from the dead, thou shalt be saved. For with the heart man believeth unto righteousness; and with the mouth confession is made unto salvation.*
> ***(Romans 10:9,10)***

Pray this prayer from your heart today!

Dear Jesus, I believe that You died for me and rose again on the third day. I confess that I am a sinner and I'm in need of Your love and forgiveness. I repent of my sins, and from this day forward I denounce Satan, sin and the world; I accept only You into my heart.

My friend, locate a Bible-teaching, believing, Spirit-filled church and be baptized in water by immersion in Jesus' Name, expecting to be filled with the Holy Ghost.

PRAYER REQUESTS

Let me agree with you in prayer concerning your need!

> *Again I say unto you, That if two of you shall agree on earth as touching any thing that they shall ask, it shall be done for them of my Father which is in heaven.*
>
> ***(Matthew 18:19)***

Pastor Profit,
Please pray for these areas:

____

____

____

Name ______________________________________
Address____________________________________
City ____________________ State____ Zip______
Phone (____) ________________

Clip and Mail to:
Living Epistles Christian Center
P.O. Box 390467
San Diego, CA 92149-0461

Bibliography

King James Bible

The Amplified Bible (Zondervan)

W.E. Vines Expository Dictionary

Spirit Filled Bible

Scripture Index